LAFAYETTE

D0621227

This Book is a Gift of:

FRIENDS OF THE
LAFAYETTE LIBRARY

Contra Costa County Library

A Murder of Crows

CONTRA COSTA COUNTY LIBRARY

WITHDRAWN

3 1901 04144 2080

Heinemann Library
Chicago, Illinois

Richard and Louise Spilsbury

© 2003 Heinemann Library
a division of Reed Elsevier Inc.
Chicago, Illinois

Customer Service 888-454-2279

Visit our website at www.heinemannlibrary.com

All rights reserved. No part of this publication may be reproduced or transmitted in any form or by any means, electronic or mechanical, including photocopying, recording, taping, or any information storage and retrieval system, without permission in writing from the publisher.

Design by Ron Kamen and Celia Floyd
Originated by Dot Gradations Ltd
Printed in Hong Kong, China by Wing King Tong

07 06 05 04 03
10 9 8 7 6 5 4 3 2 1

Library of Congress Cataloging-in-Publication Data
Spilsbury, Louise.
  A murder of crows / Louise and Richard Spilsbury.
     p. cm. -- (Animal groups)
Summary: Describes the physical characteristics, behavior, habitat, and life cycle of crows.
  ISBN 1-4034-0742-8 (HC)   1-4034-3284-8 (PB)
  1. Crows--Juvenile literature. [1. Crows.] I. Spilsbury, Richard,
1963- II. Title.
  QL696.P2367 S65 2003
  598.8'64--dc21
                              2002004034

Acknowledgments
The author and publishers are grateful to the following for permission to reproduce copyright material:
p. 4 Laurie Campbell/NHPA; p. 5 Paal Hermansen/NHPA; pp. 6, 17 R. Wilmhurst/FLPA; p. 7 Helio and Van Ingen/NHPA; p. 8 D. Maslowski/FLPA; p. 9 Mark Bowler/Oxford Scientific Films; p. 10 St. Meyers/OKAPI/Oxford Scientific Films; pp. 11, 27 William Paton/NHPA; p. 12 John Hawkins/FLPA; p. 13 Richard Brooks/FLPA; p. 14 Gareth Hunt; p. 15 Miles Barton/Nature Picture Library; p. 16 Mike Birkhead/Oxford Scientific Films; p. 18 John Geralach/AA/Oxford Scientific Films; p. 19 Carlos Sanchez Alonso/Oxford Scientific Films; p. 20 Peggy Heard/FLPA; p. 21 Elio Della Ferrera/Nature Picture Library; p. 22 GT Andrewartha/FLPA; p. 23 Scott Camazine/Oxford Scientific Films; p. 24 Derek Robinson/FLPA; p. 26 Tim Zurowski/Corbis; p. 29 E.A. Janes/NHPA.

Cover photograph of rooks in a tree, reproduced with permission of NHPA/EA Janes.

The publishers would like to thank Claire Robinson for her assistance in the preparation of this book.

Every effort has been made to contact copyright holders of any material reproduced in this book. Any omissions will be rectified in subsequent printings if notice is given to the publisher.

Some words are shown in bold, **like this.** You can find out what they mean by looking in the glossary.

Contents

What Are Crows? 4

What Is a Flock of Crows Like?. 6

What Is a Roost Like? 9

Where Do Crows Live? 11

What Do Crows Eat? 13

How Smart Are Crows? 17

Do Crows Talk to Each Other? 20

How Do Flocks Care for Their Young? 22

What Dangers Do Crows Face?. 26

Crow Facts 29

Glossary 30

More Books to Read 31

Index. 32

What Are Crows?

Crows are birds. There are 116 **species** of crows, including ravens, rooks, jackdaws, and magpies. Crows are all quite large birds, as big or bigger than pigeons. They have fairly long beaks, and they are all intelligent. This book mostly discusses three of the most common crows—the **carrion** crow, the hooded crow, and the common, or American, crow.

Carrion, hooded, and common crows

Carrion crows and common crows look alike. They have black feathers and legs, a heavy black beak, and large feet. The hooded crow is similar to carrion crows and common crows, but it has some gray feathers.

Carrion crows are usually about 18 inches (45 centimeters) long from beak to tail and weigh about a pound (half a kilogram). When they fly, they flap their strong wings quite slowly.

4

What is a bird?

Birds are animals that have wings. Their bodies are covered in feathers and they lay eggs. Birds have **adaptations** that help them fly. Their bones and feathers are light, but strong, and they have powerful muscles to flap their wings.

Group life

Crows are **social** birds and they spend a lot of their time doing things with other crows, such as sleeping or feeding.
A group of crows is often known as a flock, although its real name is a murder. People in the past probably gave this unpleasant name to crow groups because they sometimes feed on dead animals. Their black color may have reminded people of death.

This is a murder, or flock, of crows. Although each crow is an individual and does things by itself, it spends part of its life in a group like this one.

What Is a Flock of Crows Like?

Most of the time, crows live in flocks of up to fifteen birds. These flocks are often made up of members from the same family. At the center of the family are a male and a female crow who usually stay together for their whole lives. The other flock members are mostly the sons and daughters of the central pair of crows.

The family is not together all the time. Just like a human family, individual members go off on their own or in smaller groups. Crows may split up for hours, days, or even weeks while they search for food.

A pair of male and female crows spends a lot of time near each other, sometimes even helping each other to **preen** feathers that are difficult to reach.

Know your family

● ● ● ● ● ● ● ● ● ●

To us, crows may all look alike. But a crow can tell which crows belong to its flock because it can remember what they look like and what their calls sound like.

What is life in a flock like?

In a flock of crows, there is a **pecking order**. This means that some crows are more important than others. The most important crows are the oldest males. These are the **dominant** birds. Next come the younger males, and then the females. Dominant male crows are usually the ones that start fights with crows from other flocks and find nesting places or food.

Some young crows stay with their parents for five years or more. When a young male crow finds a female to **mate** with, the new pair often returns to live near his parents. Young females usually leave for good. This is because a female's flock would fight any males from other flocks with whom she might mate.

Crows can easily spot other crows, even if they are far away. Their black color stands out against the daytime sky.

7

A flock's year

Family flocks tend to remain apart from other crows during the spring and summer months. This is when crows have their young. Families are busy making nests and taking care of baby birds. There is lots of food at this time of year, so there is enough for crows to eat and to feed their young.

In the cold months of fall and winter, there is less food available. Crows have to travel farther and spend more time looking for their food. At night they gather together with other flocks of crows in **roosts.** A roost is a place where lots of birds rest or sleep, usually on one tree or on several trees close to each other.

Rooks are crows that nest together in big groups of about 50 nests. In some parts of Europe, "crow cities" have been seen with up to 16,000 nests.

What Is a Roost Like?

A crow roost is a very noisy place where groups of hundreds or even tens of thousands of crows gather at night. Crows from many different flocks sometimes meet in groups of trees where crows have gathered every winter for years.

Every evening at sunset, the crows appear at the roost, flying in from all directions. After some squawking, they all find places to rest and go to sleep. In the morning, they leave again to find food. They usually leave and return by the same route each day.

How do crows sleep?

After settling down in a roost, a crow, like this jackdaw, often **preens**. It then tucks its beak under its feathers and squats down on a branch.

Why come to a roost?

Crows stay in **roosts** partly to protect themselves from night **predators**, such as owls. If a predator attacks a bird, then it or one of its neighbors will cry out with an warning **call**. This gives the others a better chance of escaping danger than if they had been sleeping alone.

Many scientists believe that crows also share information at their roosts. They pass on information in the calls they make, but also in the way they act. For example, crows may all follow one crow, usually a **dominant** male that has found a good food source. This is especially important in winter when food is hard to find.

Although a roost of crows can be spotted more easily than a smaller group, crows are safer if they stay together.

Where Do Crows Live?

Crows live in lots of different **habitats**, from windswept mountains to city streets. Many crows prefer open spaces, and some like high landing places with good views from which to look around. The common, or American, crow is found throughout most of North America. **Carrion** crows and hooded crows live in parts of Europe, Asia, and the Middle East.

The reason that crows can live in so many different habitats is that they can eat almost anything and **adapt** to the surroundings almost anywhere. They deal with changes in their environment by finding new places to live. For example, in areas where forests have been cut down to build towns and cities, crows build nests at the top of telephone poles instead of in trees.

In towns and cities, crows, like the carrion crow shown here, use walls as lookout posts to watch for food and enemies.

11

What is a crow's territory?

In the **breeding season,** pairs of crows mark out part of the **habitat** they live in as their own. This area is their **territory.** Within the territory the crows can find the food they and their family will need and a safe place to nest. Territories are bigger in places where there is less food because the crows have to travel farther to get all they need to eat.

Crows **call** from different parts of their territory to tell other crows it is theirs. They chase away any crows from other flocks that come into their territory. These birds are a danger because they might try to take the flock's food, eat the flock members' eggs, or even kill their chicks.

We cannot see where one crow territory ends and another begins. The territories do not have fences around them like the fields of neighboring farms.

What Do Crows Eat?

Crows are **omnivores**. They eat both animals and plants. They are not fussy about whether they eat meat from animals they kill or **carrion**. In fact, crows eat just about anything they can find or catch—grasshoppers, caterpillars, worms, **grubs**, grain, berries, mice, the eggs and young of other birds, and garbage. If there is not much food nearby, crows will fly for up to 30 miles (50 kilometers) in a day to find enough.

Crows are able to eat so many different foods partly because of their beaks. A crow's beak is strong enough to crack open tough seeds and shells. It is also long and sharp enough to probe about in soil to find and catch wriggling **prey**. After the crow has found food, it uses its strong feet to hold the food while it eats it.

Crows, like this hooded crow, that spend some time near the seashore eat crabs, mussels, and clams as well as other food.

13

Getting the food they want

It is not just because crows eat anything that they are able to live in different **habitats**. They also find ways to make use of what is available to them in ways that many other animals do not. They wash sticky or muddy food before they eat it. They drop shelled animals, such as clams, from great heights to crack the shells so they can eat the animals inside. People have seen hooded crows using their beaks and feet to pull up fishing lines and steal the fish caught on the end.

Using tools

Some crows use tools to help them get food. If a crow hears **grubs** moving inside branches or beneath leaves on the ground, it may find a twig with a curved end. Using its beak like a knife, the crow removes the bark and leaves. Then it carves the twig into a sharp hook to stick into the leaves and catch the grub. New Caledonian crows, like the one in this picture, sometimes carry the tools they have made to other feeding places so they can use them again.

People have seen **carrion** crows using cars to crack walnuts for them. The crows wait at traffic lights and when the cars stop, they fly down and place walnuts in front of the cars. After the cars have driven over the nuts and the traffic has stopped again, they swoop down to collect their meal!

Why feed in a flock?

Living in a flock is a good way to get enough food. If a bird feeds on its own, it has to spend quite a lot of time looking up and checking for danger. If it does not keep watch like this, it may be hurt or killed by a **predator.** In a flock, each bird can depend on others to do the checking for some of the time, so it can spend more time feeding.

Crows in this flock take turns to feed while others act as lookouts.

16

How Smart Are Crows?

When a crow **hatches** out of its egg, it already knows how to do some things. It knows it must open its beak and squawk to get food if its parents come to the nest. It also knows that it should sit quietly in the nest for the rest of the time so as not to attract predators. The young crow quickly starts to learn other things, such as what its family members look like and, eventually, how to use its wings to fly.

Crows learn quickly. Young crows learn how to feed chicks in the nest by watching their parents do it.

Crows are particularly smart birds because they learn a lot by copying other crows in their flock. For example, if one bird figures out how to open clams by dropping them on rocks, other flock members soon learn how to do the same thing by copying.

Learning to avoid danger

One of the most important things crows learn is to recognize and avoid danger. Some crows have learned that a human holding a stick is not a threat, while a human holding a gun is to be avoided at all costs.

Amazing memories

One of the reasons crows are so smart is that they have good memories for certain things, such as where food is. They often sit like guards at the top of telephone poles or trees, watching what is going on. If they see other birds carrying twigs or food to nests, they remember their location. Then they alert other crows in their flock so they can all fly back to the nests for a meal of eggs or chicks.

Can you fool a crow?

Cuckoos are birds that lay their eggs in the nests of other birds. When they hatch, cuckoo chicks throw the other birds' eggs or chicks out of the nest. However, one type of crow, the azure-winged magpie, shown here, has learned that cuckoo eggs look different from their own and throw the cuckoo eggs out of their nests!

Crow maps

Crows seem to carry maps of their **territories** in their heads. One North American crow, the Clark's nutcracker, collects over 30,000 seeds in the fall and buries them in different parts of its territory. This territory can stretch for over 115 square miles (300 square kilometers), but in the winter the crow remembers where nine out of every ten seeds are buried!

This Clark's nutcracker lives in Rocky Mountain National Park in Colorado. These birds can remember which area they buried seeds in months before.

Do Crows Talk to Each Other?

Humans **communicate** not just by talking or writing, but also in the way we look and the things we do. Crows use movements that mean something to other crows, too, but they communicate mostly by using special **calls.**

Crows use different calls to mean different things. Most of their 25 calls sound like "caws" to us, but they are all different. Some are longer or louder than others. These differences change the meaning of the call. For example, one kind of call is used to gather the family together and another is used to let others know when a crow needs help.

Crows make different calls for different **predators.** They make one call if a cat is near and a different kind of call if a hawk is closing in.

Attracting a mate

Male crows, like many other male birds, have a special **display**. A display is a dance or series of movements that they use to tell a female that they want to **mate** with her. If they don't get it right, the female might choose to mate with a different male.

This male pied crow is bowing for a female, in order to get her attention.

To attract a mate, a male crow spreads his wings and tail and fluffs his feathers up. He bows to the female and struts around, while making a call that sounds a bit like a rattle. He also shows off his flying skills by zooming into the air, diving, and turning sharply. If the female is interested, she approaches him and they often **preen** each other.

Copycats

Crows learn how to communicate by copying other crows. Some crows, such as jackdaws, become very good at copying other animals. They can even learn to imitate cat meows!

When crows are ready to **mate,** they build a nest. A nest is not usually a bird's home. They build it just to lay their eggs and care for their young.

Baby birds grow inside an egg outside their mother's body. Eggs need to be protected from **predators** and from cold. Parent birds keep eggs warm by covering them with their warm, feathered bodies.

Nest building

A pair of crows makes a new nest together each year in spring, somewhere within their family's **territory**. First they build a rough basket out of sticks and twigs. They then smooth the inside using mud, grass, moss, hair, or feathers. This makes it softer and helps keep the wind out so the eggs and the parents won't get too chilly.

This jackdaw is collecting hair from a horse's back to use in its nest. Crows take about two weeks to collect all the materials they need for their nests.

The early days

Both parents usually take turns keeping the eggs warm. Crow chicks **hatch** out of the eggs after about eighteen days. They are blind and have few feathers.

While they are in the nest, the young birds depend on their parents, and sometimes their older brothers and sisters, to bring them food and to remove their droppings. The chicks grow quickly. After a few days, their eyes open and their first feathers appear. After four or five weeks, all their feathers are fully grown and they have enough strength to fly.

A female common crow lays between three and six bluish, blotchy eggs at a time.

Washing worms

Crow chicks get the water they need from their food. Dry food, such as bread or dried worms, might be too dry and choke crow chicks. So, adult crows dunk the food in puddles of water before feeding it to them.

Crows often nest near other crows. This helps them spot **predators** more quickly. But more predators are also attracted to the noise of so many crows.

Growing up

Most young crows stay with their families for about three years. In this time, their parents usually **mate** a few times, so family flocks can have up to fifteen members. Young crows help by finding nest materials or food for their parents.

After three years, young crows find partners of their own. They nest in or near their parents' **territory**, especially if the territory contains lots of food. Those who live in territories with little food often move to completely new places, where there may be more food.

Survival

Predators often eat crow eggs. If that happens, a pair of crows will mate again to replace the young. On average, fewer than half the eggs laid survive to become adult crows. Crows can live for up to eight years.

The older brothers and sisters in a flock sometimes act as baby-sitters, caring for the chicks and bringing them food while the parents are away feeding.

What Dangers Do Crows Face?

Just like humans, crows argue now and then, and arguments can turn into fights. Fights are more likely when there is not enough food to go around and when it is time to **mate**.

Within a family flock, fights are usually short and are limited to a few pecks and loosened feathers. **Dominant** males often fight other male family members over who is most important. Sometimes, however, they just **call** and fly around in a flashy way. This **display** reminds the others how well the dominant male might fight if he had to, without actually having to fight.

Fighting other crows

Fights with other flocks of crows are different. Crows fly at others they spot in their **territory** and will try to peck and claw them to death. Sometimes they lock claws as they fight and tumble around in trees and on the ground.

Their speed, strength, sharp beaks, and claws make crows good fighters.

Predators

Birds of prey, such as owls and vultures, are **predators** that eat crows. Animals that climb trees, such as squirrels, raccoons, and snakes, also try to snatch and eat eggs and crow chicks from their nests. Crows change their nesting places each year so predators cannot learn where they are. Some even build a false nest in one place before building their real nest elsewhere.

To defend themselves, crows often get together and **mob** attackers. If a crow sees a predator, it makes an alarm call and any crow from the flock that hears comes to help. Crows sometimes help crows from outside their flock if they are in trouble. By doing a favor for another flock, they might be helped themselves in the future.

When crows mob a predator like this eagle, they rarely actually peck it. Instead, they shout at the predator or chase it away.

27

People problems

Some people do not like crows. They can be a problem for farmers, because they steal hens' eggs and sometimes damage crops. When they eat farm animals that have died, some people mistakenly think the crows have killed them. When they gather in **roosts** in large numbers, crows are noisy and their droppings are messy. Because of these problems, some people hunt and kill crows.

In many countries there are laws to stop people from harming these smart birds. Farmers use other ways to keep crows off fields, such as scarecrows. If a roost is becoming a problem, people sometimes use recordings of crow warning **calls** to frighten the crows away.

What is good about crows?

Crows can actually help farmers grow crops. They eat the **insects** that would otherwise eat the crops. They can also help clean streets by eating leftover human food and **carrion** from animals that were killed by cars.

What's the largest crow?

The largest type of crow is the raven, whose body is up to 26 inches (66 centimeters) long. That's about the size of a small vulture. The jackdaw, the smallest crow, is half the size of a raven.

Crow sayings

The lookout point on the highest part of a ship is called a "crow's nest." This is because crows often build their nests high up in tall trees or on telephone poles, where they can get a good view of other crows and also of **predators.**

Crow funeral

Crows sometimes gather by the hundreds around a dead crow. All the crows go quiet, then suddenly fly away together.

Pretty things

Crows, especially magpies, like to find shiny objects, such as bits of mirror or metal, silver paper, and even jewelry. They often build collections of these shiny items in tree holes or old nests.

Glossary

adaptation special feature that allows living things to survive in their particular habitat

bird of prey bird that hunts and kills other animals for food

breeding season certain time of year in which a type of animal mates

call sound, or group of sounds, made by an animal

carrion meat from an animal that is already dead; also, a type of crow

communicate pass on information to another

display put on a show of actions that sends a message to another animal

dominant refers to the leader or most important member of a group of animals

grub young insect without wings, also called a larva

habitat place where an animal or plant lives in the wild

hatch break out of an egg

insect small, six-legged animal with a body divided into three sections: head, thorax, and abdomen

mate joining of a male and female of the same species to create young

mob when a group of crows chases away an animal, such as a vulture

omnivore animal that eats both animals and plants

pecking order order of importance of animals in a group. The highest member in the pecking order is the leader.

predator animal that hunts other animals for food

preen to clean dirt and insects out of feathers to keep the feathers healthy

prey animal that is hunted and eaten by another animal

roost place where birds rest or sleep, usually on the branches of a tree

social living in well-organized groups of animals that work together

species group of living things that are alike in many ways and can mate to produce young

territory particular area that an animal or group of animals claims as its own

More Books to Read

Frost, Helen. *Bird Families*. Bloomington, Minn.: Pebble Books, 2000.

Kirkland, Jane. *Take a Backyard Bird Walk*. White Plains, N.Y.: Alliance House, Inc., 2001.

Kress, Stephen W. *Bird Life*. New York: St. Martin's Press, LCC, 2001.

Latimer, Jonathan P., and Karen Stray Nolting. *Backyard Birds*. Boston: Houghton Mifflin, 1999.

Nathan, Emma. *What Do You Call a Group of Turkeys?: And Other Bird Groups*. Farmington Hills, Mich.: Blackbirch Press, 2000.

Pascoe, Elaine. *Birds Use Their Beaks*. Milwaukee: Gareth Stevens, 2002.

Pringle, Laurence. *Crows!* Honesdale, Penn.: Boyds Mill Press, 2002.

Robinson, W. Wright. *How Birds Build Their Amazing Homes*. Farmington Hills, Mich.: Blackbirch Press, 1999.

Stewart, Melissa. *Birds*. New York: Scholastic Library, 2001.

Index

adaptations 5, 11

beaks 4, 13, 26
birds of prey 27

calls 6, 10, 12, 20, 26, 28
carrion 13, 28
carrion crow 4, 11, 15
chicks 12, 17, 23, 25, 27
Clark's nutcracker 19
common (American) crow 4, 11, 23
communication 10, 20–21
crow funeral 29
"crow's nest" 29
cuckoo 18

dangers 10, 12, 16, 17, 18, 20,
    22, 24, 27
displays 21, 26
dominant birds 7, 10, 26

eggs 22, 23, 25

farm 28
fights 7, 26
flock (murder) of crows 5, 6, 7,
    8, 16, 25, 26
food 8, 10, 12, 13–16, 18, 23, 25

group life 5, 6–8, 10, 16

habitats 11, 14
hooded crow 4, 14

intelligence 4, 14, 15, 17, 18

jackdaw 4, 21, 22, 29

life span 25

magpie 4, 18, 29
mating 7, 21, 22, 25
memories 18, 19
mobbing 27

nests 8, 11, 22, 23, 24, 25, 27
New Caledonian crow 14

omnivores 13

pecking order 7
predators 10, 16, 17, 20, 22,
    24, 25, 27, 29
preening 6, 9, 21

raven 4, 29
rook 4
roosts 8, 9, 10, 28

size 4, 29
species of crows 4
stealing 28, 29

territories 12, 19, 22, 25, 26
tools 14

young crows 7, 8, 17, 25